Chat Room for Teens 1

Introduction

The Chat Room is a wonderful invention. It allows users instantly to communicate freely, and for free, with anyone in the world. They can talk about any subject they care to, and express their opinion in any way they like. They can even be in contact with many people at once. The Chat Room has indeed revolutionized global communication.

CHAT ROOM FOR TEENS operates in much the same way. English learners are encouraged to express themselves freely on a wide range of relevant topics. Many thought-provoking questions and examples are given to spur independent language usage. There are no specifically "right" or "wrong" answers, so there is no need for users to be intimidated — any more than if they were discussing the same topics in their own language instead of English. And this natural, interesting teaching method will build confidence as well as competence, helping the learners to master a skill that will have countless applications — social as well as commercial — around the world, for the rest of their lives.

English, after all, is actually Earthlish — if Dutch, Korean, Saudi, and Brazilian colleagues meet together in Moscow, they will undoubtedly talk to each other in English. And the ones who are best able to express themselves accurately and effortlessly will have a tremendous advantage over their less-talented fellows. Promoting this skill and facility in English is the goal and purpose of the entire line of LIS Korea books, from EXPRESS YOURSELF to TEEN TALK to any of the other fine publications by this thoughtful, progressive company.

Duane Vorhees

Contents

Lesson 1	Can I Speak to Sue?	8
Lesson 2	It Is Hot Today!	22
Lesson 3	I Have a Cold	36
Lesson 4	Daily Routine	50
Lesson 5	I Like School	64
Lesson 6	I Want to Make Many Friends	78
Lesson 7	Let's Eat Out Tonight	92
Lesson 8	I Like Sports	106
Lesson 9	We Got a New Car	120
Lesson 10	Let's Go Shopping	134

Chat Room for Teens

LESSON 01 Can I Speak to Sue?

— Warm-up Dialog —

Feeling Better

Bobby : Hi, Mrs. Jones. How are you?

Mrs. Jones : I'm very well, Bobby. How are you?

Bobby : I'm okay now. Thanks.

Mrs. Jones : Sue said you were sick.

Bobby : Yes, I had the flu. I had to miss a week of school.

Mrs. Jones : Well, I'm glad you feel better now.

Chat Room for Teens

Bobby : May I speak to Sue?

Mrs. Jones : I'm sorry, she isn't home now. She's still in ballet class.

Bobby : When do you think she'll be back?

Mrs. Jones : She said she was going shopping first. So maybe she'll be home in two or three hours.

Bobby : May I call back then? Or can she call me?

Mrs. Jones : Of course! Can I pass along a message?

Bobby : Just tell her I need some help with all the homework I missed.

• Questions

1. What is Sue's complete name?
2. Where is Sue? What is she going to do next?
3. Why is Bobby calling her?

Pictures

1.

   Q1: What does "Hang on" mean?

   Q2: When would someone use that expression?

   Q3: What other, similar, expressions could you use instead of "Hang on please"?

2. Q1: What does "You've got the wrong number" mean?

   Q2: When would someone use that expression?

   Q3: If someone told you you've got the wrong number, what would you say? What would you do?

3.

   Q1: When do people use this expression?

   Q2: If you were asking someone to take a message, what would you say?

   Q3: We do not hear this expression much anymore. Why not, do you think?

Talk

4. **Q1:** What are some differences between talking and texting?

    Q2 How often do you text? Who do you usually text to? Who do you usually talk to?

    Q3: Which method of communicating do you think is more convenient? Why?

5.

    Q1: Do you often get spam? How many spam messages do you get per week?

    Q2 How do you cope with it?

    Q3: Why do people send spam? What do you think about them?

6. **Q1:** Do you use the internet on your phone? Why or why not?

    Q2 What do you use the internet for most of the time?

    Q3: If you use the internet on your phone, how much does it cost? Is that a reasonable fee?

LESSON 01 Can I Speak to Sue?

Answer Me

1 An Important Question

Stella : Hi, Dad.
Dad : Hi. What's up?
Stella : I have an important question to ask.
Dad : OK. What do you want to know.
Stella : Well, can I get a new phone?
Dad : Why? Is there something wrong with the one I got you a few months ago?
Stella : No. It's fine.
Dad : Then why do you need a new one?
Stella : All my friends are getting new ones. They laugh at the one I have. They say it's old-fashioned.
Dad : But you picked it out yourself.
Stella : I know. But fashions have changed. I need to keep up.
Dad : But it'll change again in a few more months, and then again a few months later. I can't just keep buying you a new phone all the time!
Stella : I know. But, just this once, okay?
Dad : No, I don't think so.
Stella : I knew you would say that!

Dad! Let me show you something for just a second.

Questions

1. Which one do you agree with more, Stella or her father?
2. Do you have a phone? How long have you had it? How many phones have you had in the last two years?
3. Do your parents always buy you a new one when you ask for it?

Chat Room for Teens 01

• 2 Sound Policy

Teacher : Whose phone is that ringing? Is that yours, Tommy?

Tommy : Yes, sir. I'm sorry.

Teacher : Give it to me!

Tommy : OK. Here it is. Can I have it back at the end of class?

Teacher : No, you know what the rules are. I'll give it back to you in a month.

Tommy : A month! That's not fair.

Teacher : But you know what the rules are.

Tommy : But this is my first offense. I just forgot to turn it off this time, because nobody ever calls me anyway.

Teacher : Then, since you never use it, you won't miss it for the next month, will you?

Tommy : But I need it to call other people. And I have to let my parents know where I am.

Teacher : But the rule is, if a phone rings in my class I keep it for a month. I can't treat you any differently than anyone else who has broken this rule, can I?

• Questions

1. Do you think the teacher is being fair? If you were the teacher, what would you do?
2. Do you usually take your phone to school? What are the school rules about doing so?
3. What do your parents think about your having a cell phone?

LESSON 01 Can I Speak to Sue?

— Answer Me —

• 3 Privacy Or Responsibility

Mom : Ralph! Who is Ronnie?
Ralph : He's a friend. Why?
Mom : Why do you need to call him so often?
Ralph : We have a lot to talk about.
Mom : Ten times a day?
Ralph : Maybe. But how do you know how many times I talk to him?
Mom : I looked at the record of calls on your cell phone.
Ralph : Mom! That's not right! This is my private business. It isn't any of your concern who I talk to or how many times. Or even what we talk about!
Mom : No, I'm your mother. I have a responsibility to watch over you.
Ralph : But I'm not doing anything wrong! I'm just talking to my friend, that's all!
Mom : But I don't know that. That's why I asked you. I want to make sure you aren't in trouble.

• Questions

1. Who is right? Why?
2. Have you ever had a similar experience? What happened? What did you do?
3. Do you ever want to see other people's phone records? Why or why not?

Chat Room for Teens 01

• 4 Letter From Dad

Michael : I got a wonderful surprise today.
Joan : What was it?
Michael : I got a letter from my dad.
Joan : A letter? Did he go someplace?
Michael : No, he's right here, just like every day.
Joan : Then why did he send you a letter? What did it say?
Michael : Oh, nothing special. He just wanted me to know that he loves me.
Joan : Doesn't he ever tell you that at home?
Michael : Of course he does!
Joan : Then why did he send you a letter to tell you that?
Michael : I don't know, but I think it's sweet. It's very special. It's not like getting an ordinary text message or a phone call.
Joan : Hmmmmmm. Maybe I should write a letter to my mom and tell her how much she means to me. I bet she'll be surprised!

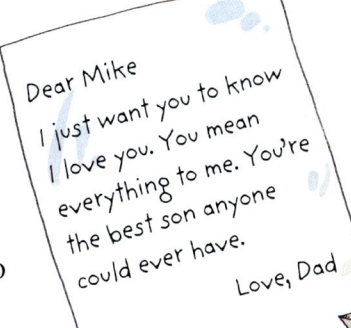

• Questions

1. Why do people seldom write letters any more?
2. Have you ever written a letter to a friend? What kind of message did it contain?
3. Do you have a pen pal?

LESSON 01 Can I Speak to Sue?

—— Let's Talk More ——

- **1 No Call Back**

I called Frank yesterday. I needed to find out if he has a sweater I lost. I think it's at his house. But he didn't answer my call, and he didn't call me back. So I sent him a text message, and he didn't respond to that, either. Now I'm very angry at him. I think he should have called me back. That's just common courtesy, don't you think? I'm sure he's deliberately ignoring me for some reason. What should I do?

- **Questions**

1. Would you be angry if something like this happened to you? Explain your answer.
2. If someone calls you or leaves a text message, do you always call back?
3. What are some possible reasons why Frank didn't answer or call back?

Chat Room for Teens 01

● 2 Disconcerting

I went to the concert last night. The musicians were wonderful! But people in the audience were not so terrific. Every few minutes, somebody's phone would go off, distracting me from the music. Even worse than that, sometimes those rude people would actually talk on their phones! I think this behavior is disgusting! I went to the concert to enjoy the music, but it was constantly being interrupted. I'm sure the musicians were just as upset as I was, too. I can't understand how anyone can be so discourteous in public.

Who's paying attention to what?

● Questions

1. Do you always turn your phone off or put it on vibrate when you are in a public place?
2. Why should people in public respect the privacy of others?
3. How do you behave if other people bother you with their private calls in public? Do you ask them to be quiet or just ignore them?

LESSON 01 Can I Speak to Sue?

— Let's Talk More —

• **3 Thumbs Up! Or Thumbs Down!**

Easier to call!

Youngsters have grown so skillful at sending text messages that they are now called "thumbsters." It even seems that they can communicate better with their thumbs than with their tongues. But older people have a lot of trouble using the new technology. They are very clumsy with their thumbs, so they are not very fast or accurate. Many of them try to compensate by using their fingers instead. But even doing that is hard for them. So, even though it costs more, they would rather communicate the old-fashioned way: using their phones to talk into instead of typing on.

Cheaper to text!

• **Questions**

1. Why are some people called thumbsters? (What two English words are being combined?)
2. Why do older people have trouble sending text messages?
3. How did people use their phones to communicate in the past? Do people still do that?

4 Home Phone

I don't understand why anybody still has a regular phone at home. We have one, even though everyone in my family has a mobile phone of his own. My father has two mobile phones! But we still have the old-fashioned phone in the living room. I know it costs money every month, but we keep it anyway. I wonder why.

Questions

1. What reasons would someone with a mobile phone want to keep a home phone as well?
2. Do you use your home phone often? Why or why not?
3. Why would some people have more than one mobile phone?

LESSON 01 Can I Speak to Sue?

Real Talk

That Man!

Jim : Did you hear that man?

Sally : Sure! Everybody heard him! How could anyone be so rude?

Jim : I know. I really didn't want to know so much about his private business.

Sally : Me, neither. I thought it was really embarrassing.

Jim : I don't really care about what he did last night.

Sally : I know. Why can't people show a little courtesy toward others?

Jim : They shouldn't talk so loud into their cell phones.

Sally : Or they should try to find a more private place.

Jim : Sometimes it's hard to get off the subway to do that.

Sally : I know, but he could have tried to go between the cars. Or at least he should have talked more quietly, or called back when he was alone.

He's making too much noise!

• Questions

1. Where are Sally and Jim now, probably?
2. Why do they think the man on the phone is rude?
3. How could he have shown more courtesy to others?
4. What would you do if you saw someone acting like that?

Chat Room for Teens 01

Read Me

I Want A Phone

Parents don't know what to do about a modern technology fad. Their kids keep asking for mobile phones of their own, and many parents are reluctant to buy them. They worry about the expense, of course, and they are afraid that their children will lose them or break them. In addition, parents think phones interfere with studying. There is also a lot of concern about some adults who use cell phones to stalk innocent children. Most of all, parents suspect that kids are merely reacting to peer pressure: they don't have any real need for a cell phone, but they want one because "all" of their friends have one.

Nobody will talk to me if I don't have a phone.

● Questions

1. Do you think parents should buy a mobile phone for a very young child? How old should a kid be before he has a phone of his own?
2. What happens if a parent says no?
3. What do your parents think about your having a phone? Did they gladly get you one, did you pressure them into getting you one, or don't you have one?

LESSON 02 It Is Hot Today!

— Warm-up Dialog —

Seasonable

Tom : This is a wonderful day, isn't it?

Jane : No, it's much too hot.

Tom : It's a perfect day for swimming.

Jane : Maybe so. But I'm afraid of the water.

Tom : Well, sometimes people just stay by the beach or poolside when they "go swimming."

Jane : I know. But I really don't like summer very much. I don't like the hot weather.

Swimming cools me off!

Chat Room for Teens

Tom : So I guess you like winter instead?

Jane : Yes! I love to ski! Have you ever tried?

Tom : No. I don't like cold weather at all. But my favorite time of the year is the fall.

Jane : Yes. I like the colors and the warm days and cool nights. But, except for winter, I like the spring best.

Tom : Not me. The weather is too unstable, and it rains too much. The only thing I like about spring is that it means winter is over.

Nothing beats downhill!

● Questions

1. What does Tom like to do in hot weather?
2. What is Jane's favorite sport?
3. What are the good qualities of spring?

Pictures

1.

   Q1: What's the weather like?

   Q2: What do you like to do when the weather is like this?

   Q3: Do you know how to stay cool when it's hot outside?

2. Q1: What's the weather like?

   Q2: What should you have when you go out in this weather?

   Q3: Do you like this kind of weather? Why or why not?

3.

   Q1: What's the weather like?

   Q2: Do you like winter? Why or why not?

   Q3: Which do you like better, skating, skiing, or snowboarding? How often do you get to do those things?

Talk

4.
- Q1: What's the weather like?
- Q2: Where does "yellow dust" come from? What causes it?
- Q3: What do you do when the yellow dust comes?

5.

- Q1: What's the weather like?
- Q2: Are you afraid of thunder and lightning? Why or why not?
- Q3: Every year we have monsoons. Do you like that time of year? Talk about the good and the bad effects of a monsoon.

6.
- Q1: When summer is almost here, what do you think about?
- Q2: What do you do during summer vacation?
- Q3: Which do you like better, summer or winter? Explain your answer.

LESSON 02 It Is Hot Today!

— Answer Me —

• 1 Don't Forget Your Umbrella

Mom : It's raining outside. You'd better take an umbrella.

Jeff : I don't think so. It's only raining a little bit and will probably stop soon. And I'd probably forget I had the umbrella with me and lose it.

Mom : I'm afraid you're going to get soaked and catch a cold. If you forget your umbrella, it's okay.

Jeff : No it isn't! You told me the same thing last week, and then you got angry with me when I didn't bring it home.

You can't go out without an umbrella!

• Questions

1. Do you always take an umbrella with you on a rainy day? Do you like to walk in the rain?
2. Which do you prefer, an umbrella or a raincoat?
3. How often have you lost an umbrella? What did your parents say about it?

2 To Swim Or Not To Swim

Steve : Let's go swimming! It's too hot.

Anne : I hate it when there are too many people in the pool. I'd rather just stay at home and take a shower.

Steve : Oh, come on! The swimming pool isn't so crowded.

Anne : All right, to be frank with you, I can't swim! I'm afraid of the water.

Steve : Don't worry. I'll teach you how to swim. Just hurry up!

Questions

1. Can you swim? When did you learn?
2. How often do you go swimming?
3. Have you ever thought you were going to drown? Talk about your experience.

LESSON 02 It Is Hot Today!

Answer Me

- ### 3 Why Isn't A/C OK?

    Ellie : Dad, it's getting hot. Why don't we buy an air conditioner this summer?

    Dad : Air conditioning is expensive. An electric fan works just as well, and it's healthier.

    Ellie : I don't think so. Electric fans only give out hot wind.

    Dad : But it is natural and good for your health. Just take a shower and you will feel cool with an electric fan.

Questions

1. What does "Air conditioning is expensive" mean?
2. Do you have an air conditioner in your home? If so, how often do you use it?
3. Do you know why the father thinks air conditioners might not be good for Ellie's health?

Chat Room for Teens 01

• 4 Snow Fun

Jim : It's snowing. Let's go out and make a snowman and have a snowball fight!

Denise : No way! My mom hates it when my clothes get dirty.

Jim : My parents don't think it matters. They even play with me in the snow.

Denise : You're so lucky! I wish my parents would change their mind.

I told you not to get your new clothes dirty!

• Questions

1. Do you like the snow? What do you do when it snows?
2. Do your parents ever go out and play with you when it snows?
3. Do you think adults like snowy weather? Why or why not?

LESSON 02 It Is Hot Today!

Let's Talk More

1 Chill Out

People have different ways of staying cool in summer. Some take a shower several times a day, and some go to the swimming pool. Others stay indoors with the air conditioner constantly on. My friends tell me that eating ice cream and drinking cold water helps a lot. But in my experience, I just think how cool it is, regardless of the real temperature, and I'm fine.

It's broiling!

Questions

1. What do various people do when it is hot?
2. What is your suggestion for staying cool?
3. Do you understand what "I just think how cool it is, regardless of the real temperature" means? Put the phrase into your own words.

2 Open The Windows!

I think it's time we open the window and let some fresh air in. We've stayed in this air-conditioned room for the last five hours. Haven't you heard that we should ventilate an area every two hours when the air conditioner is on? Otherwise, the air gets stale, and the cooling chemicals can make us sick.

Questions

1. Do you think using an air conditioner is good or bad for one's health? Why do you think so?
2. What are the most important things to remember about using an air conditioner?
3. Which is more comfortable, using an electric fan or an air conditioner? Why?

LESSON 02 It Is Hot Today!

Let's Talk More

- **3 Who Loves A Rainy Day?**

When it rains, most people feel blue. The sky is dark and depressing, and the air is wet and cold. But some people love rainy weather — especially cab drivers! They get a lot of extra business on days like that.

Every cloud has a silver lining!

- **Questions**

1. Do you feel blue when it rains?
2. Why do people tend to hate the rain?
3. Other than taxi drivers, who else likes it?

Chat Room for Teens 01

• 4 How Many Seasons?

Like most other countries, Korea has four distinct seasons. Some countries, however, only have one or two seasons. For instance, near the equator it's always hot, but there is usually an obvious rainy season. At the poles, the weather varies between really cold and not so cold — and during the winter there is no sunlight at all, while during the summer there's no night time!

Why not six or seven seasons?

• Questions

1. Name the four seasons. In what months do they occur?
2. How is weather different at the poles and along the equator?
3. Describe the weather today, in detail.
4. Some meteorologists say the climate of Korea is changing. Do you know why?

LESSON 02 It Is Hot Today!

Real Talk

Taking A Walk

Dick : I'm tired of staying in all day. I'm going out for a walk.
Mom : But it's raining.
Dick : No, I think it's stopped. Or at least it's only sprinkling a little bit.
Mom : Okay, you go to the store for me. I need some vegetables.
Dick : Sure. Can I keep the change?
Mom : All right. But don't spend it all on something foolish. And come right back home, I need those veggies right away.
Dick : I'll just be gone a few minutes.
Mom : Don't forget to take an umbrella.
Dick : Aw, Mom! Do I have to? I don't need an umbrella. It's hardly raining at all.
Mom : I don't want you to get wet. You'll catch cold.
Dick : No, I won't. It's pretty warm, and it's not raining hard enough to get me wet. Especially since I'm only going to the store.
Mom : I don't care. I don't want you to get wet at all. I'm worried about acid rain.
Dick : You know I always lose umbrellas. I set them down for just a minute, and then I forget all about them. I bet I've lost a dozen of them this year!
Mom : That's okay. If you forget it this time, you can just go right back to the store and get it.

I told you so, didn't I?

• Questions

1. What does the mother want?
2. What does she want her son to do?
3. Why doesn't he want to take an umbrella?
4. What does "acid rain" mean? Are you afraid of it? Why?

Chat Room for Teens 01

Read Me

The Value of A Weatherman

We don't need a weatherman to tell us if the sun is shining right now. But knowing what the weather is probably going to be like later today, or over the next few days, is very useful. If it is probably going to rain, we might want to postpone going on a picnic. If a typhoon is coming, we should keep away from the beach area. And being stuck on a mountain during a snowstorm can be very dangerous. I know some people make fun of the meteorologists because they are not always right, but the science of weather forecasting is pretty accurate nonetheless, thanks to weather satellites and a lot of close analysis of weather patterns. Besides, if I want to know if it's going to rain, I just ask Grandpa. His left arm always hurts before a storm.

Who is more accurate?

• Questions

1. Why do people make jokes about weathermen?
2. What difference does it make if we know the weather in advance?
3. Is Grandpa a meteorologist?

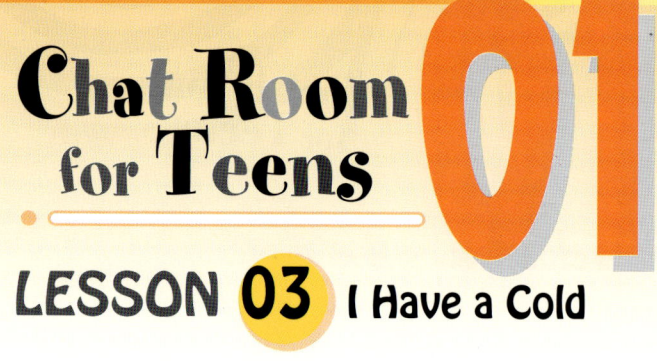

Chat Room for Teens

LESSON 03 I Have a Cold

Warm-up Dialog

Not Feeling Well

Mom : Jerry, wake up, you're going to be late.

Jerry : Mom, I don't feel well. I don't want to go to school.

Mom : What's wrong?

Jerry : I have a bad cold. I feel like I have a fever, I can't stop coughing, and my nose keeps running.

Mom : Okay, then I will call your teacher. But you still need to get up. We have to go see the doctor.

Chat Room for Teens

Jerry : Oh, I don't think I need a doctor. I'll be fine if I just stay in bed some more.

Mom : No, you need to get an antibiotic shot to cure your cold.

Jerry : No, no. I'll be fine, really. I know how much trouble it is for you to take me to the doctor. Just let me rest and play some video games, and I'll be fine.

Mom : Do you really have a cold? Or are you just trying to stay home from school?

Jerry : What?

• Questions

1. In what ways does Jerry feel sick?
2. What does he think will cure him?
3. What does his mother think he needs to do to feel better?

Pictures

1.

Q1: What is happening in the picture?

Q2: How do you know if someone has a fever?

Q3: Have you ever had a fever? What did your parents do?

2. Q1: What's wrong with the boy?

Q2: Why is his mom angry?

Q3: Do you ever eat late at night? Why or why not?

3.

Q1: What is happening?

Q2: Why do you think the boy is bleeding?

Q3: Do you know how to deal with a nosebleed?

Talk

4.
- Q1: Do you regularly see a dentist? Why or why not?
- Q2: Do you feel comfortable when you visit a dentist?
- Q3: How often do you brush your teeth? Do you always brush your teeth when you go to bed?

5.

- Q1: What's wrong with the boy?
- Q2: How often do you have a cold? What are symptoms of the common cold?
- Q3: What do you do when you get a cold?

6.
- Q1: What is your opinion about going to a hospital?
- Q2: Do you like shots? Do you like taking medicine?
- Q3: Do you think doctors and nurses are kind?

LESSON 03 I Have a Cold.

— Answer Me —

- **1 What's Wrong With Having Too Much Fun?**

    Jerome : Mom, I have a stomach ache.
    Mom   : Didn't you have a good time at your friend's birthday party?
    Jerome : Yes, but I ate too much.
    Mom   : Do you want to go see the doctor?
    Jerome : No, I will just walk a while. That will help me feel better.

Maybe something was wrong with the pizza!

- **Questions**

    1. Do you often have stomach aches?
    2. What do you do when you have one?
    3. Do you usually eat a little bit or a lot?

2 Screening Problem

Jacob : My eyes hurt. I don't want to go to school.
Mom : What did you do last night?
Jacob : I just talked with my friends on the internet.
Mom : How late?
Jacob : Until early this morning, I guess.
Mom : I warned you about using the computer too much. It isn't good for your eyes.

Too much eyestrain!

Questions

1. How often do you use the internet? How long?
2. What do you usually do on the internet?
3. Do you think looking at a computer screen too long can hurt you?
4. What do your parents think about how you use a computer?

LESSON 03 I Have a Cold.

— Answer Me —

- ### 3 Abrasions

    Dad : What happened? You have cuts and bruises all over!
    Doreen : I fell down while riding my bike.
    Dad : You should be more careful. A lapse of concentration leads to accidents.
    Doreen : I know. And it hurts!
    Dad : Want to see a doctor?
    Doreen : No, my bruises will heal of themselves in a couple of days.

My knees are not beautiful anymore!

- ### Questions

    1. Can you ride a bike well?
    2. Do you usually see a doctor for cuts and bruises? Why or why not?
    3. Do you always wear protective gear when you ride a bike? Why or why not?

Chat Room for Teens 01

• 4 Extraction

Tabitha : Dad, I think I need to have my tooth pulled out. It aches a lot.

Dad : It serves you right. I've told you and told you to brush your teeth after every meal. But you never want to listen to me.

Tabitha : But what about my toothache?

Dad : I'll make a dental appointment for you.

Ow!

If I don't brush my teeth, pretty soon I won't have any left!

•Questions

1. What do you think about going to a dental clinic?
2. When you go to a dentist, do you feel different than when you go to a doctor?
3. Do you use a regular tooth brush or an electronic or sonic one? What's the difference among them?

LESSON 03 I Have a Cold.

Let's Talk More

- **1 A Testing Time**

    Sometimes kids get so worried about upcoming exams that they get headaches. Even if they have spent a lot of time preparing for their tests, they are anxious because their parents might be disappointed in the scores. Handling stress can be very difficult emotionally, especially for young people.

I'd rather play baseball!

- **Questions**

    1. Do you get headaches as exam time approaches?
    2. Do you study every day, or do you cram just before a test?
    3. Are your parents sensitive about your test results? What would happen if your grades were lower than they expect?

Chat Room for Teens 01

• 2 Not A Wink

I saw my friend yesterday and asked why she looked so tired. She said she hadn't slept a wink the night before. She was awake because her younger sister had a high fever and cried all night. The whole family stayed awake all night. When I asked how her sister was feeling, my friend said she didn't know, because she's still in the hospital.

• Questions

1. When was the last time you went to a hospital? Why did you go?
2. Have you ever gone to the emergency room? If so, why? What was it like?
3. Why do people need to go to the emergency room? (Who goes there?)

LESSON 03 I Have a Cold.

— Let's Talk More —

- **3 Sore Throat**

    I still have a sore throat, and it's getting worse. My mom told me last week I should see a doctor about it, but I resisted. I was sure that it would get better if I just ignored it. Now I wish I had listened to her. I can't see a doc soon enough! I hope he doesn't have to operate.

- **Questions**

    1. Do you often get sore throats? When?
    2. What do you do to get relief?
    3. Do you rush to see a doctor, or do you just rest and take medicine at home?

Chat Room for Teens 01

• 4 No More Eggs!

Sally had to miss school today because she ate a couple of boiled eggs. She isn't sick because she ate too much, and I don't think anything was wrong with the eggs, because I had some too and I feel fine. So I guess she must be allergic to eggs.

I want fried chicken, not eggs!

• Questions

1. Allergies display many kinds of symptoms. Can you name any of them?
2. Are you allergic to anything?
3. Are there any kinds of food that you can't eat or hate eating? What are they? Why don't you like them?

LESSON 03 I Have a Cold.

Real Talk

A Fevered Situation

Doctor : What's wrong with you today?

Christy : I have a fever.

Doctor : Okay, let's see. Open your mouth and push your tongue down on the thermometer.... Yes, you're right. You have a high temperature. Just relax here for a few minutes while I prepare some medicine and a prescription. Just take some rest when you get home and drink lots of water, and I'll see you again the day after tomorrow.

Christy : Sir, I don't have to get a shot, do I? I'm afraid of needles.

Doctor : My nurse gives excellent shots. You won't feel a thing, I promise.

Christy : No, please! I'm scared!

Doctor : Okay, maybe your fever isn't too high. I'll just prescribe some additional medicine and see you tomorrow instead.

Christy : Whew! Thanks a lot!

Open wide!

● Questions

1. What's wrong with Christy?
2. Did Christy get a shot? Why or why not?
3. When is her next appointment?
4. What did the doctor say to Christy about his nurse?

Chat Room for Teens 01

Read Me

Stay Well

Doctors recommend simple steps to avoid disease:

1. Wash your hands often, at least 8 times a day, using soap.
2. Work out at least a half hour three times a week.
3. Maintain a balanced diet (don't eat much fast food or instant food, and don't overeat).
4. Get a medical check-up twice a year.
5. Rest when you are tired.
6. Get plenty of sleep (eight hours a day is preferred, and certainly more than six hours a day). If you nap during the day, keep it short (less than an hour).
7. Laugh as often as possible. Laughter is the best medicine.

Pay close attention!

Questions

1. How often do you wash your hands?
2. How often do you work out?
3. What happens if you eat too much?
4. How often do you get a medical check-up?
5. What happens if you keep working when you are tired?
6. How many hours do you sleep every night?
7. What makes you laugh?

Chat Room for Teens 01

LESSON 04 Daily Routine

— Warm-up Dialog —

On A Treadmill

Diane : I feel like I'm in a rut.

Joe : Me too. It's the same thing every day.

Diane : I get up early every morning and take a bath. Then I eat breakfast and go to school.

Joe : That's exactly what I do, too, except I take a shower after breakfast.

Diane : And then I spend all day in school.

I feel like a hamster in a cage!

Chat Room for Teens

Joe : School might be kind of fun if I could spend more time with my friends instead of listening to the teacher so much.

Diane : And then I have to go to a music studio to learn how to play the piano.

Joe : You're lucky! I have to go to an academy to study some more. I wish I could learn taekwando instead, or play football with my buddies.

Diane : When I finally get home, I eat supper.

Joe : After supper, I still have homework to do.

Diane : I know. Me too.

Joe : If I'm really lucky, I finish early enough to play a game on my computer. But then I have to go to bed right away.

Diane : And then the next day it's the same schedule all over again.

Joe : Life is so boring!

● Questions

1. What is a "rut?"
2. Describe Joe's typical day.
3. How is Diane's day different than Joe's?
4. Describe your daily routine.

Pictures

1.
   - Q1: What's happening here?
   - Q2: Is it easy for you to get up early in the morning? Who wakes you up?
   - Q3: What time do you usually get up? How about on weekends?

2.
   - Q1: Do you take a shower every morning?
   - Q2: Do you brush your teeth after every meal and also before you go to bed?
   - Q3: Do you follow the three-minute rule when you brush your teeth? Why or why not?

3.
   - Q1: Do you like school? Why or why not?
   - Q2: Do you study hard in school? Why or why not?
   - Q3: Do you think your studying will give you a better future?

Talk

4.
- Q1: What is happening in this picture?
- Q2: Why do you think his mom is angry?
- Q3: Do your parents nag you often? About what?

5.

- Q1: Do you often help your parents with chores at home? What do you do?
- Q2: Do you sometimes get extra allowance for helping your parents?
- Q3: Have your parents ever asked you not to help? What was the reason?

6.
- Q1: Do you like to talk on the phone? Do you text?
- Q2: Which is more convenient, text messaging or talking on the phone? Explain your answer.
- Q3: Do you ever argue with your parents about the phone bill?

LESSON 04 Daily Routine

— Answer Me —

- **1 Get Up!**

    Mom   : Wake up! It's already seven o'clock.
    Chris : Mom. It's Sunday. We don't have any class today.
    Mom   : I don't think it's good to sleep late, even on a weekend.
    Chris : I'm tired, and the weekend is the only time I can get enough sleep!

- **Questions**

    1. Do you get enough sleep during the week?
    2. Can you sleep as late as you want on weekends? Why or why not?
    3. Do your parents sleep late on weekends?

Chat Room for Teens 01

• 2 Studying Can Be Fun

Ian : I hate to study. I just want to play with my friends.

Anne : Playing is good, but studying is also enjoyable.

Ian : No way! How can studying ever be fun?

Anne : Because if you study hard, you can understand how things work, so then you can avoid a lot of problems.

• Questions

1. Do you like to study? Why or why not?
2. Do your parents force you to study?
3. Why do you think we should (or should not) study hard?

LESSON 04 Daily Routine

— Answer Me —

• 3 In Charge

Jasmine : Where are you going?

Daniel : I'm going to the supermarket to buy some bread and fruit.

Jasmine : Why?

Daniel : My parents are out, and I promised them I'd take care of my little sister.

• Questions

1. Are your parents busy? Do they go out often?
2. Have you ever taken care of your younger brothers or sisters?
3. Do your parents appreciate what you do for them?

Chat Room for Teens 01

• **4 Singing In The Smoke**

Warren : Mom, I'm going out tonight.

Mom : Why? Where are you going?

Warren : We're going to a karaoke after my friend's birthday party.

Mom : I don't want you to go. Adults smoke a lot there, and I'm afraid you will suffer from second-hand smoke.

Without any adults around, we can have fun and be ourselves!

• **Questions**

1. Do you like to sing at a karaoke?
2. What do your parents think about your going there?
3. Are you worried about second-hand smoke?

LESSON 04 Daily Routine

— Let's Talk More —

• 1 Eating Disorder

My parents worry too much about what I eat. I love hamburgers and pizza, but they won't let me eat them more than once a week. I know they care about my health and they want me to have a good, rounded diet. But I should be able to have what I like, too.

• Questions

1. Do you like fast foods such as hamburgers and pizza? How often do you eat them?
2. What do your parents think about fast food?
3. Do they always cook for you? Do they sometimes order out? How often do you go to a restaurant?

• 2 Don't Skip

When people think they are gaining weight, they may be tempted to skip meals. But this is rarely a good idea. We need a constant intake of food, at regular intervals, to stay healthy. A much better idea is to eat less at each meal, to maintain a good balance between the kinds of food we eat, and to get more exercise. Some experts suggest that eating very small meals more often (five or six times a day) is the best practice of all.

• Questions

1. Do you eat three meals every day? Do you ever have additional snacks?
2. Do you work out often?
3. Are you worried about your health?

LESSON 04 Daily Routine

Let's Talk More

• 3 No Conditions

I don't like having a conditional allowance. It's nice to be rewarded for getting good grades or for helping out around the house, but I don't think my allowance should be based on those things. I should get a set amount, no matter what. And then, if my parents feel like they want to reward me, that's all right, too!

I'd rather be safe than sorry!

• Questions

1. Is your allowance conditional?
2. How much do you get? Do you think that is enough?
3. What do you do if you ever need more money?

Chat Room for Teens 01

• 4 Too Early?

I have a 6 o'clock curfew, so I never get to have much fun with my friends. I've complained about this to my parents, but they never take my reasoning seriously. I think their parents must have had strict curfews too, and so my parents are exacting their revenge on me!

What a stupid curfew!

• Questions

1. Does your family have a curfew for you?
2. Do you think kids should have one?
3. Why do adults get to stay out as late as they like?

LESSON 04 Daily Routine

Real Talk

Problems Solved

Frank : I'm sick of this routine. I want a change!

Mom : I'd like a change, too. I'm tired of all your complaining.

Frank : Just to be different, I think tomorrow I'm going to stay in bed late.

Mom : No, you won't. You have to go to school. But I'll let you go to bed early tonight so you won't be tired.

Frank : And no more showers! I hate showers.

Mom : Then you can take a bath instead.

Frank : But the bathtub is too small!

Mom : That's your problem. It's either going to be a shower or a bath. I'm not going to let my son go to school dirty and smelly.

Frank : And I'm tired of the same old breakfast every day. I want some toast and milk.

Mom : Good. It sounds like something that you can make for yourself without much trouble. You'll be saving me a lot of work. But make sure you wash your own dishes too.

Frank : I'm going on strike, effective immediately. No more studying!

Mom : Instead of complaining so much, you ought to be studying right now. I think you need to cut back on your play time and start doing more homework.

Frank : Mom, you don't understand. I'm bored with my life. I want a change!

Mom : Okay. We'll add an hour of exercise every day. That will be a good change, don't you think?

Questions

1. What does "going on strike" mean?
2. What does "effective immediately" mean?
3. Frank and his mother both want to change Frank's routine. How do they differ in what changes they want to make?

Chat Room for Teens 01

Read Me

A Little Spice

People without a regular routine every day soon get tired of the uncertainty, so they look for more stability. But most of us follow a regular schedule instead, and we need to look for something new and exciting that will relieve the boredom. It isn't so hard to do, actually. We can have different meals. Sometimes we can eat before showering and shower before eating at other times. Maybe we can vary the way we go to school or work, though we don't have much control over what time we need to be there. It's always possible to change the way we look or dress and the people we spend time with. None of these changes is very radical, but taken together each will help add some spice to our otherwise boring lives.

Too much spice leads to heartburn.

• Questions

1. If we "add spice" to our routine, does that mean we add salt or pepper? What do we really mean by that expression?
2. What kinds of changes are easy to make?
3. What is the difference between people who are in a rut and people who do not have a regular routine?

Chat Room for Teens 01

LESSON 05 I Like School

— Warm-up Dialog —

Model Life

Lisa : I hate school.

Dad : When I was a student, sometimes I hated it too. But it wasn't all bad.

Lisa : What did you like about it?

Dad : Well, I liked being with my friends. Some of them are still very close to me to this day.

Lisa : But I like being with them better when we're not in school. Then we can do what we want to do.

Oh, school is so uncool.

Chat Room for Teens

Dad : I always enjoyed the challenge of learning new skills. I wouldn't be where I am today in my profession without them.

Lisa : But I'm going to be a model. Models don't need to know math!

Dad : They do if they're not going to be cheated by their agents. They also need to learn to enjoy reading a good book, because they sit around for many hours with nothing to do.

Lisa : And I hate my teachers. They're too strict. And they assign too much homework.

Dad : Well, you have a point there, I guess. But aren't there some teachers that you like? I've heard you say some pretty good things about your English teacher.

Lisa : Oh, he's all right, I guess. But I wish he taught something more interesting and more useful than English.

• Questions

1. Why doesn't Lisa like school?
2. Do you think any of her points are valid? Tell us why.
3. Does her father agree with her? Why or why not?

Pictures

1.

Q1: What subjects do most kids study in school?

Q2: Do you know why kids today need to study so many things?

Q3: Which is your favorite subject? What subject do you hate the most? Why?

2.

Q1: Are you ever late for class? How often? Why?

Q2: Have you ever been absent from school? Why?

Q3: Do you sometimes hate going to school? What would you do instead?

3.

Q1: Did you ever have an argument with any of your friends? What was it about?

Q2: Did you then make up again? How?

Q3: Do you usually apologize when you think you are wrong?

Talk

4.
- Q1: Do you like school lunches? Why or why not?
- Q2: What is your favorite food?
- Q3: Do you care about how many calories you consume? Why or why not?

5.
- Q1: What is happening?
- Q2: Does your school have a field day every year?
- Q3: Did you ever compete for your class on field day? How well did you do?

6.
- Q1: Have you ever thought about joining Boy Scouts or Girl Scouts? What decision did you reach? Why?
- Q2: Talk about the Scouting objectives, as you understand them.
- Q3: What can people learn in Scouts?

LESSON 05 I Like School

— Answer Me —

• 1 Good Teacher?

Andy : What do you think about your new teacher?

Betty : He is very strict with us in the class. But he becomes friendly and loving after class. I'm very confused.

Andy : He has a good reputation among students. He wants to see them study hard and accomplish their dreams.

Betty : But I want him to be friendly and loving in the classroom too. It might be better.

Two-faced?

• Questions

1. Talk about one of your teachers. Is he or she friendly or strict?
2. Does that teacher ever discipline you? How? Do you agree or disagree with his or her methods?
3. What have you learned from that teacher?

Chat Room for Teens 01

● **2 Mathematical Certainty**

Melinda : I hate math! I don't understand why we have to learn it.

Dad : That's interesting. I liked it very much when I was in school.

Melinda : Really? I don't believe you. I can already add, subtract, divide, and multiply. That should be enough math for anybody!

Dad : Unfortunately, that's not enough. Higher math helps us develop our logic and reasoning ability. And there's only one right answer!

● **Questions**

1. Do you like math? Why or why not?
2. Why is it important to learn math in school?
3. Do you know how people can improve their math skills?

LESSON 05 I Like School

— Answer Me —

- **3 Class Act**

    Alex   : I can't wait until the next English class! I like it very much.
    Bonnie : Really? I'm confused. There are too many irregular verbs.
    Alex   : Yes, it's hard to learn at first. But I like my English teacher.
    Bonnie : Why?
    Alex   : She is Jamaican and very friendly. She tries to encourage me and is always ready to correct my mistakes without making me feel stupid.

How can we make friends with English?

- **Questions**

    1. Do you like English? Why or why not?
    2. Are you afraid of speaking English?
    3. How do you study English? Do your parents help you? Do you go to a language institute?

Chat Room for Teens 01

- ### 4 No More Phone

    Alice : I tried to call you. Why didn't you answer me?

    Dilbert : I'm sorry. My mom took away my phone.

    Alice : Why? What did you do wrong?

    Dilbert : Nothing, really. But when she got me the phone, I promised to get better grades.

    Alice : We got our report cards last week. What happened?

    Dilbert : Well, my grades were about the same, so Mom said I broke my promise.

    Alice : Is there anything I can do to help you study?

Not until you improve your grades!

Questions

1. Should the possession of a mobile phone depend on something beyond Dilbert's ability?
2. Who was wrong initially, Dilbert or his mom, in setting the conditions? Or, was nobody wrong?
3. When your parents got a phone for you, did they attach any conditions? What were they?

LESSON 05 I Like School

— Let's Talk More —

• 1 The Best Policy

My teacher has a great attitude towards discipline. He says, "Be honest, and I will forgive you for anything you've done. But if you lie, watch out!" I think that's a very fair and just approach. All we have to do is be honest. Honesty guarantees no punishment under any circumstances. But if we do something wrong and then lie about it, we just make matters worse.

Does honesty guarantee a happy life?

• Questions

1. Do you agree with the teacher's rule?
2. What seems to be the attitude of your teacher?
3. What is your parents' approach towards discipline?

2 Why Play?

Like many other kids my age, I'm forced to spend many hours a week taking piano lessons and then practicing at home. I wish I had musical talent, but I know I don't have any, so I'm just bored. My mother insists that I continue, however. She tells me that someday I'll be glad I can play well. "It will help you in the future," she says. "If you stop now, you'll regret it later." I know she wanted to take lessons when she was a girl, but her family couldn't afford them. So, she wants me to have the opportunity that she missed. I'm sorry about Mom, because she is naturally musical and probably would have been a very gifted pianist, but I'm not talented in that area at all.

Questions

1. What do you do after school?
2. Do you participate in after-school activities voluntarily, or do your parents push you into them?
3. What activity are you the most interested in?

LESSON 05 I Like School

— Let's Talk More —

• 3 Envious Friend

I'm very envious of my best friend. He is not only athletically gifted, but he also gets good grades and is extremely popular with everyone. He tries to reassure me, telling me that I'm smart and good-looking, and that I too have many friends. But he's just being nice, because he's my friend. I know that I only get average grades and that I'm too shy to have a lot of friends. But it's nice to have one who is such a good friend!

He is a smart jock!

• Questions

1. Do you have many friends? Describe them.
2. Do you think you are popular in school? Why do you feel that way?
3. What is the difference between kids who are popular and those who aren't?

4 Famous Label

Yesterday I saw Sally. She was wearing new jeans with a famous designer brand. I thought they looked wonderful on her and told her so. I also told her that my parents wouldn't buy me designer clothes; they think that "famous labels" don't add anything to the clothes that they are on — except the price. I was surprised to find out that her parents feel the same way. But she saved money out of her allowance until she had enough money to buy them on her own. So I'm going to try to do that, too. I wonder how long it will take until I have enough to get some cool jeans like hers.

I'll save up for my jeans!

Questions

1. Do you like to wear top-brand clothes? Why or why not?
2. Do your parents like you to wear them?
3. Do you think it is worth paying so much money for a brand name?

LESSON 05 I Like School

— Real Talk —

Busy Work

Doris : I wish I could go see a movie with my friends right now.

Dad : You might be able to do that this weekend, but not tonight. You have too much to do.

Doris : I know! That's the problem!

Dad : What's the problem?

Doris : I have too much to do! I have too much homework and too many subjects at school.

Dad : I felt the same way when I was your age.

Doris : But I also have to take piano lessons and go to the gym every day.

Dad : Those activities should be fun, don't you think?

Doris : And I have to read so many books! I can't even find time to chat freely with my friends! This isn't any fun at all!

Dad : Well, being a student is your job right now. I'm overworked, too, you know. Everybody is busy in modern life, so you might as well get used to it.

Run! Run! Run! How busy modern life is!

• Questions

1. Does Doris like being so busy? Explain why or why not.
2. Is her dad busy also?
3. What would Doris rather do with her time?

Chat Room for Teens 01

Read Me

Different Lives

Do American students have to spend as much time studying as Korean students? The lives of Korean and American kids are different in many ways. They both spend about the same number of days in school, and their time in class is very similar too. They even study the same subjects for the most part. But American classes are usually smaller and more interactive. Discussion is more common than lectures. The real difference, though, is what they do when class is finished for the day. Many Americans are involved in what are called "extra-curricular activities." These voluntary projects may be playing sports or a musical instrument, or painting or doing community work. So kids often stay at school an hour or two after class. But then they usually go home and do whatever homework they have but are still able to spend a lot of time with their friends or watch television or play computer games. They have very free lives compared to their Korean counterparts. But they also score lower on the regular standardized tests. They waste a lot of time having fun, when they could be setting up the foundations of their lives. What both cultures need is to be a bit more like the other, so American kids could become better students, and Korean kids could enjoy their childhood more.

I'm free to play.

I'm oppressed by books.

• Questions

1. Compare an American kid's lifestyle with yours.
2. What are the advantages of each way of doing things?
3. What are the disadvantages of each way?

Chat Room for Teens 01

LESSON 06 I Want to Make Many Friends

— Warm-up Dialog —

Perfect Friends

John : I feel so lonely.

Mom : Why don't you go out and make some friends?

John : Because no one is like me. It's hard to relate to people that you don't have anything in common with.

Mom : What do you mean?

John : Well, I actually like to read and study. Learning new things is a wonderful experience. But nobody else my age seems to think so.

Mom : I'm glad that you're that way, but that doesn't make the others bad people.

John : They say they want to play sports instead, but they don't really want to exercise or develop their skill. They only want to have fun. So they aren't very challenging to play against.

Mom : But that doesn't mean you can't have fun together, does it?

What's wrong with all my friends?

Chat Room for Teens

John : And I'm beginning to find out that they lie to me, and they don't have any sense of fairness or justice. And they never keep their promises. That's why I don't like to spend any time with them.

Mom : Well, maybe you need some new friends. But don't expect too much of other people. Nobody's perfect, you know. We all have our faults, but we all need to be tolerant of each other if we're going to have any friends.

John : Then what's the point of having friends if they always let us down?

Mom : Maybe you're being too judgmental. You complain an awful lot for someone who isn't perfect either.

John : Why? What faults do I have?

Mom : I don't think you want me to list them all. But we can start with the fact that your room is always messy.

• Questions

1. Why does John think he doesn't have any friends?
2. Is he a good athlete, do you think? A good student? Why do you think that way?
3. Besides being messy, what other faults do you think John has? Are they really faults?

Pictures

1.

- Q1: What kinds of kids are popular in your class?
- Q2 What could you do to be more popular than you are?
- Q3: Do you and your friends like sports? Do you play any musical instruments? Can you sing well?

2.

- Q1: Would you like a bookworm as a friend? Why or why not?
- Q2 Do your parents want you to have bookworm friends? Why or why not?
- Q3: Do you think grades are important in friendship? Why or why not?

3.

- Q1: Are there any bullies in your class?
- Q2 What do you and your friends think about them?
- Q3: How do you and your friends cope with them?

Talk

4.
- **Q1:** When it is your birthday, who do you invite (and not invite) to your party?
- **Q2** Where do you usually have a birthday party? At home or somewhere else? Why?
- **Q3:** What would you want your friends to give you on your birthday? What do you want the most?

5.

- **Q1:** How many of your friends have mobile phones? Do you?
- **Q2** Do you think people who don't have a mobile phone feel isolated? Or are there advantages, such as privacy, in not having one?
- **Q3:** If you didn't have a phone, how could you talk with your friends?

6.
- **Q1:** Are you always on time for appointments? What about your friends?
- **Q2** Do you get angry when your friend is late? Why or why not? Does it depend on the circumstances?
- **Q3:** What can you do to make sure you are always on time?

LESSON 06 I Want to Make Many Friends

— Answer Me —

• 1 Making Friends

Elizabeth : I want to make many friends, but I don't know how.

Dad : It's easy and simple.

Elizabeth : What can I do?

Dad : Just be a friend to someone, and he or she will be your friend too.

• Questions

1. Do you want to have as many friends as possible? Why or why not? Is it better to have a few really close friends, or a lot of friends you don't know very well?
2. Do you have any idea about how to make friends?
3. Have you ever stopped being friends with someone? Why?

Chat Room for Teens 01

• 2 Heavy Topic

Candace : Dad, I'm going to skip every supper from now on!

Dad : Why?

Candace : You know. I'm getting too fat, and people don't want to have a chubby girl as a friend.

Dad : Nonsense! Do you think that's fair? Don't you think the way people look is less important than the way they are?

Candace : I don't think it's right, but it's reality!

The scale's wrong!

• Questions

1. To have friends, do you think looks are really more important than character or personality?
2. Do you do anything to stay slim? Is it easy to do?
3. "What is not seen is more important than looks." What does that mean?

LESSON 06 I Want to Make Many Friends

Answer Me

- ### 3 His Fault!

    Mom : How is your friend, John?

    Herb : I don't know. We're not speaking.

    Mom : Why not?

    Herb : We had an argument. I think he was wrong, but he won't apologize.

    Mom : I think he is a good boy, and it doesn't always matter who apologizes first. Why don't you tell him you are sorry and see what happens?

Both are waiting for an apology!

- ## Questions

    1. Do you ever have arguments with your friends? About what?
    2. Do you always apologize if you think you are wrong? What about if you don't think you are wrong, do you still apologize?
    3. Do you always accept your friend's apology?

Chat Room for Teens 01

• 4 Foreign Friends

Alice : Do you have any foreigner friends?

Bert : Yes, I have two. One is American and the other is Filipino. We are about the same age.

Alice : How did you meet them?

Bert : They just moved into my neighborhood last week.

Alice : How can you talk with them?

Bert : They are very friendly, and I enjoy talking with them in English. But I'm also teaching them Korean!

We're global buddies!

• Questions

1. Do you have any foreign friends or pen pals? How did you meet them?
2. Are they different from your Korean friends?
3. What have you learned from them? How have you helped them?

LESSON 06 I Want to Make Many Friends

— Let's Talk More —

• 1 Does Sex Matter?

Some boys only want male friends, and some girls only want female friends. They think that friends of the same sex are easier to understand and get along with. But a few kids like to have lots of friends of both genders; they think they can learn more about people if they mix with many different personalities.

Having things in common.

•Questions

1. Do you want male or female friends? Do you want both?
2. What's the difference between boys and girls, as friends?
3. What can you learn from each other?

Chat Room for Teens 01

• 2 Defining Friendship

I hear a lot of kids describe their best friends. Usually they mean some kids in their class or some neighbors. But for me, my best friends are my parents. That's right, my parents! They always try to understand me and help me. They never ask for anything in return, except for my love and loyalty. Isn't that the behavior that we ideally want our friends to exhibit toward us?

Way to go, Charlie!

• Questions

1. Who is your best friend? Describe him or her.
2. Do you think parents can be your friends? Or are parents and friends very different from one another?
3. Do your friends always behave in a friendly manner? Do you always treat your friends in an ideal way?

LESSON 06 I Want to Make Many Friends

Let's Talk More

- ### 3 Bad Influence

  I'm always fighting with my mom about one of my friends. She doesn't want me to spend so much time with him. She thinks he is a bad influence. That's because he got bad grades last semester. But he's trying to study harder, and he is always a lot of fun to be around. Somehow I've got to persuade my mother that, when it comes to friendship, grades aren't everything!

Keep away from my daughter!

- ### Questions

  1. What are your criteria for making friends? Looks? Style? Intelligence? A good personality? Moral standards?
  2. Do you think parents have a right to decide who your friends should be? Why might they think they do have that right?
  3. What would you do if your parents were opposed to your friends?

4 Does A Perfect Friend Exist?

What do you think a good friend is? Maybe you'll answer, "I know they're my friends if I have a good time with them." But I want you to be more specific. Should a friend be kind, generous, understanding, and always ready to help you when you have a problem? I'm sure you will say yes to all of those qualities. But can such a perfect friend exist? Can someone who is not perfect still be a good friend?

What is a good friend?

Questions

1. What is your definition of a good friend? On that basis, describe your friends.
2. Are you always happy with the way your friends treat you? Or do they sometimes disappoint you?
3. Are you frank with them when you are disappointed?

LESSON 06 I Want to Make Many Friends

Real Talk

Opposites Attract

Jim : I really want to be your best friend.
Janet : Me too.
Jim : But we're so different.
Janet : I know.
Jim : You hardly talk at all. You're just too shy.
Janet : Do you think so? Maybe you talk too much.
Jim : Maybe I do. But that's because I have to fill up the silence all by myself. I wouldn't have to talk so much if you talked more.
Janet : Maybe you're right. But I just never have anything interesting to say.
Jim : You should stop reading so much and get more involved with life. Then you'd have more to talk about.
Janet : Well, I don't just read books, you know. I also like to listen to music.
Jim : So do I. But not all the time! You should become more active. Maybe you could learn to play some sports.
Janet : Sports bore me. It always seems like a lot of fuss over some insignificant achievement like kicking a ball into a net or hitting a ball with a stick. It's just a sweaty waste of time.
Jim : Wow! I've never heard you talk so much!
Janet : Maybe you're just too busy talking yourself that you don't have any time to pay attention to what I say.
Jim : OK, I'll try to do better. I want to know what you think about.
Janet : OK, I'll try to do better too, so you'll know.
Jim : Just because we have different personalities doesn't mean we can't be good friends.

Let's have a talk!

• Questions

1. What adjective describes Jim's personality? Why do you think so?
2. What adjective would probably be applied to Janet? Why would people say so?
3. Why doesn't Janet like football or basketball? Why doesn't she like baseball?

Read Me

The Right Friend

Everybody wants to know how to make friends and how to tell good friends from bad ones. Some people are naturally engaging. They easily talk to people they hardly know, so even strangers usually like them immediately. But some people are more private and reserved. It is harder for them to become well-liked. First impressions do count a lot in establishing relationships, but that does not mean that only outwardly friendly people can be good friends. Many times, our best friends are people we needed a long time to get to know. Their qualities may be deeper and harder to appreciate. But, in the end, these people may turn out to be more loyal and honest than our more popular comrades. One true friend is far more valuable than a hundred superficial ones.

How can I tell?

• Questions

1. Do first impressions count?
2. In general terms, describe your best friend.
3. Are friendship and popularity the same? Why or why not?

Chat Room for Teens

LESSON 07 Let's Eat Out Tonight

Warm-up Dialog

Food Choices

Sam : Hi, Mom.

Mom : Hello, Sam. What's the matter?

Sam : Nothing's the matter. I hope it's okay to call you at work.

Mom : Sure, that's fine. But I only have a moment.

Sam : I just called to ask if it is okay for us to eat out tonight. I don't feel like staying at home.

Mom : I think that's a great idea. I have a lot to do here today, and it would be very hard for me to get home early. What would you like?

Sam : How about some pizza?

Mom : I'd rather feed you something healthier than that!

Sam : Then how about hamburgers?

Let's make a deal!

Chat Room for Teens

Mom : Sam!
Sam : Okay, okay. No harm in trying, is there?
Mom : Might I suggest a vegetarian meal? No meat or fatty food, and no calories.
Sam : And no taste, either! I might as well stay at home and eat ramyon.
Mom : Okay, let's compromise. Why don't you meet me at the Chinese restaurant next to my office? You know the one?
Sam : Of course I do. It's the same place we always eat out together.
Mom : Fine. I'll meet you there at 7:30. Don't be late!
Sam : OK.

● **Questions**

1. Where is Sam's mother? What does she do?
2. What kind of food does Sam like? What doesn't he like?
3. Why is Chinese food an "acceptable" compromise between Sam and his mother?

Pictures

1.

- Q1: Do you ever want to eat out? When?
- Q2: How about your parents? Do they want to eat out too, or just stay at home?
- Q3: What does your family usually have when you eat out?

2.
- Q1: What do you like to eat? Why?
- Q2: Do you usually eat it by yourself alone or with your friends?
- Q3: Do you think your favorite food is expensive? Or can you afford it yourself, from your own pocket money?

3.

- Q1: Do you like to buy food from street vendors? Why or why not?
- Q2: Is the food (snacks) from street vendors cheap, do you think? What are some of the prices?
- Q3: What do your parents think about the food you get from street vendors?

Talk

4.
- Q1: Today, boys and girls often have parties at fast-food restaurants. Can you guess why?
- Q2: Do you often eat at fast-food chains?
- Q3: What is your favorite fast food? What about your friends' favorites?

5.

- Q1: Do you usually have dessert after a meal?
- Q2: What is your favorite dessert?
- Q3: Is there a dessert that your parents like that you don't care for?

6.
- Q1: Are you always careful about how many calories are in the food you eat? Why or why not?
- Q2: What is your favorite food that has a lot of calories?
- Q3: What's wrong with high-calorie foods, especially, because they taste so good?

LESSON 07 Let's Eat Out Tonight

— Answer Me —

- **1 What To Eat?**

    Rihanna : I want a hamburger. Let's eat out!

    Dad : I want to eat out too, but I want to have rib soup.

    Rihanna : I hate rib soup! I like hamburger.

    Dad : How about if we get you a hamburger at one place while I go to a Korean restaurant nearby for rib soup?

    Rihanna : That's a good idea!

There is no accounting for taste!

- **Questions**

    1. When your family wants to eat out, do you usually approve of your parents' choice of restaurants?
    2. What is your favorite restaurant food? What do your parents like?
    3. Who finally decides where to eat?

Chat Room for Teens 01

• 2 Not The Same

Gary : Let's eat out for lunch, Mom!
Mom : What would you like?
Gary : How about pizza?
Mom : Okay, I will buy everything for the pizza and make it at home.
Gary : No! It doesn't taste right when you make it.
Mom : But it is less expensive and healthier.

• Questions

1. Does your mom ever bake pizza for you at home?
2. Which do you like better, brand-name pizza or the one your mom makes?
3. Do you think pizza in a restaurant is expensive? What do you think a reasonable price would be?

LESSON 07 Let's Eat Out Tonight

— Answer Me —

● **3 In Or Out?**

Mom : Let's order out. What do you want to eat?

Eric : I want sweet-and-sour pork. But let's go out to eat it instead of staying here at home.

Mom : No. I'm busy and tired. So, let's have it delivered.

Eric : But it tastes fresher in the restaurant.

People don't want to wait to eat!

● **Questions**

1. Do you like sweet-and-sour pork? How often do you eat it?
2. Do you like it better when it is delivered? Why or why not?
3. What Chinese foods do you like the most?

Chat Room for Teens 01

• 4 Some Bad Squid

Morris : Let's have some squid. I'm hungry.

Beth : I don't think so. You felt sick last week when we had it. Why don't we get something different?

Morris : Last week I wasn't feeling well, so the squid made me sick. But I'm fine now. Let's go for it.

Beth : I don't think the squid is very sanitary. That's why you had a stomach ache last week.

The squid got even!

• Questions

1. Are you afraid that the food you eat may not be sanitary?
2. Have you ever had a stomach ache after eating something in a local restaurant?
3. What foods do you eat often with your friends? Why do you eat those?

LESSON 07 Let's Eat Out Tonight

— Let's Talk More —

• 1 Lots Of Good Choices

I'd like to eat out every day! These days my parents are busier than ever. So, they could save time by not having to shop for food and fixing meals at home. And, besides, then we could vary our meals every day and choose whatever we feel like at the time. And I could avoid the yucky things my parents always make.

How to choose?

• Questions

1. Would you want to eat out every day? Why or why not?
2. Do you think your parents would like the idea of eating out all the time?
3. What are some problems with never eating at home?

Chat Room for Teens 01

● **2 What Mama Says**

Mom told me why instant food tastes so much better than normal food. The manufacturers add more salt and sugar and chemical additives to give it a stronger, better taste. These additives also make them more addictive. So she says they are not healthy. Most people don't understand the long-term bad effects of eating junk food; that's why they still crave them.

Secrets of junk food.

● **Questions**

1. Do you think instant food tastes better than regular food? Give your reasons.
2. Do your parents worry about your eating too much junk food?
3. Would you continue to eat instant food even if you knew it was not healthy?

LESSON 07 Let's Eat Out Tonight

Let's Talk More

• 3 Where To Celebrate?

Tomorrow is my birthday! I invited my friends to have a party at a fast-food restaurant. My mom wanted me to have a party at home instead, but I'd rather have it there. It seems more like an important event that way. And, besides, it would be a lot less work for her.

This way!   No, home!

• Questions

1. Will you celebrate your next birthday at home or in a restaurant? How do your friends usually celebrate?
2. Is your mother willing to prepare your favorite foods for your birthday? What are they?
3. What presents do you usually get from your parents? From your friends?

Chat Room for Teens 01

• 4 Going Dutch

I don't understand why some people prefer going Dutch. I think it's friendlier and more respectful if one person pays for the meals of his friends. But, of course, the friends need to take turns paying for the meals, or it wouldn't be fair.

Get whatever you like. But you pay!

• Questions

1. Do you understand why your parents sometimes pay the whole bill when they meet their friends or relatives in a restaurant?
2. Do you usually go Dutch when you eat with your friends?
3. If it's your birthday, do you have to pay for all the meals yourself? If so, what do your friends do?

LESSON 07 Let's Eat Out Tonight

— Real Talk —

Pizza Problem

Peggy	:	What are we going to eat tonight? I'm hungry.
Dad	:	Your mom will be back tomorrow, don't worry.
Peggy	:	That's tomorrow! What about tonight? Let's go out to eat. Please!
Dad	:	I'm sorry. I'm beat. Working all day and then coming home at night and having to do the housework here has worn me out. I'll sure be glad when your mother comes home. I couldn't take too many days like this.
Peggy	:	Does that mean you're going to cook for us?
Dad	:	No, I'm too tired to cook.
Peggy	:	That's a relief!
Dad	:	So, let's order a pizza to be delivered. What kind do you like?
Peggy	:	I like bacon and lots of cheese.
Dad	:	That sounds good. Why don't you call that pizzeria on the corner. The food should be here in just a few minutes.
Peggy	:	Why don't we call Pizza Palace instead?
Dad	:	Pizza Palace! They charge almost twice as much as the local pizzeria.
Peggy	:	But it's still pretty cheap. And it tastes a lot better.
Dad	:	You're just brainwashed by the brand. There isn't much difference between them, except for the price.
Peggy	:	No, I think Pizza Palace tastes a lot better. You're just being a Cheap Charlie!
Dad	:	I don't mind paying a lot for good quality. If Pizza Palace tasted twice as good, I'd gladly pay the difference. But since the taste is almost the same, I won't.
Peggy	:	OK, if you insist. But I think you're making a big mistake.
Dad	:	Well, if you feel that way, you can pay for it out of your allowance.
Peggy	:	But then I wouldn't have any money left for new earrings!
Dad	:	Or we could both save money, and you could cook a good meal for the two of us. The practice would be good for you.
Peggy	:	What did you say the pizzeria phone number was?

Can you see any differences?

• Questions

1. What does it mean to be "beat?"
2. What is the main difference between the pizza with the famous brand and the local product?
3. What are Peggy's choices?

Chat Room for Teens 01

Read Me

Why We Don't Eat At Home

Why do many people eat out more frequently than a generation ago? There are probably many reasons. One obvious one is that there are more opportunities now; fast-food outlets in particular are far more numerous. This is probably an outgrowth of the busy modern lifestyle, in which people spend less time at home and more time at work or play outside the house. More women have jobs and don't want to go home and then cook for their families, so they eat out. And, probably, fewer women (and men, too) learn how to cook while growing up, so they need to go to restaurants just to survive.

As fast foods become commonplace, home meals are getting exotic.

• Questions

1. Why do people eat out?
2. How does the modern lifestyle promote eating out?
3. Is it easy for people to work at home and also away from home?

Chat Room for Teens 01

LESSON 08 I Like Sports

Warm-up Dialog

Basketball Pros And Cons

Jack : Do you want to come with me?

Sarah : What are you going to do?

Jack : I'm going to play some basketball with my friends.

Sarah : Well, in that case, no thank you. I'll go with you some other time.

Jack : I thought you like basketball.

Sarah : I do. It's my favorite sport. I watch it on TV every chance I get.

Jack : But watching it on television isn't the same thing as watching it live! It's only real when you play it.

Chat Room for Teens

Sarah : Well, I don't play basketball, but I still love it.

Jack : Then why don't you come watch me play?

Sarah : On TV, the camera people always focus on the most exciting thing that's happening, and the announcers always have interesting comments to make.

Jack : So?

Sarah : But when I watch you and your friends play, I just get bored. There's no one else to talk too, and you guys don't make many baskets. The pros are sure a lot more exciting to watch.

● Questions

1. Does Sarah like to play basketball? Explain your answer.
2. Does Jack like to watch basketball? Why do you think he does (or does not)?
3. Why doesn't Sarah want to watch Jack play?

Pictures

1.

Q1: Can you roller skate? Do you use in-line skates?

Q2: How often do you roller skate? With whom do you skate? Where do you skate?

Q3: Do you often fall down and hurt yourself? Do you always wear protective gear?

2. Q1: Can you swim? When did you learn? Who taught you?

Q2: Why should people learn how to swim, do you think? Or, is it not important to know?

Q3: What benefits does swimming provide?

3.

Q1: Do you know taekwondo? Is it hard to learn?

Q2: Do you think taekwondo is good for self-defense? What other benefits might it have?

Q3: Do you like martial arts (such as taewkondo, boxing, wrestling, karate, or judo)?

Talk

4.
- Q1: Do you like to ski? How well do you ski?
- Q2: Do you often fall down? Are you afraid of skiing?
- Q3: Who taught you how to ski? Was learning difficult?

5.

- Q1: Do you have a bicycle? How long have you had it?
- Q2: How often do you ride it?
- Q3: Are your parents worried about your riding a bicycle due to traffic?

6.
- Q1: What do people do in fitness centers?
- Q2: Why do you think people exercise?
- Q3: Have you ever gone to a fitness center? Describe your experience.

LESSON 08 I Like Sports

— Answer Me —

• 1 Getting There

Bob   : I want to go to the movie, but I don't have any way to get there.

Janet : It's only three blocks from here. Why don't you just walk?

Bob   : It's too far!

Janet : It will only take about 15 minutes to get there.

Bob   : Are you sure?

Janet : Of course, I walk there all the time.

Bob   : Really?

Janet : Yes. Lately I've been doing a lot of walking. It's cheap, easy, and good for my health. And I never have to feel helpless because I can't go somewhere.

Why not walk?

• Questions

1. What does Bob want to do? Why doesn't he do it?
2. What is Janet's suggestion?
3. How far away is the cinema?

Chat Room for Teens 01

• 2 Sporting Life

Jason : When I grow up, I'm going to be a famous athlete.

Maureen : Really? What sport do you want to play?

Jason : Football, of course. It's the greatest sport in the world!

Maureen : Well, good luck! You're going to have to be extremely good to play professional football. Everyone wants to do that, and only a tiny number ever make it.

Jason : I know. But I have a fall-back plan, just in case I can't play football for a living.

Maureen : What's that?

Jason : I'll switch to golf! I'd probably have a longer career in that sport because it's not as physically demanding.

Maureen : But it's very expensive to practice!

Jason : Yes, that's right. But I think I could do well at it.

Maureen : Have you ever golfed?

Jason : Well, no, but I've watched it a lot on TV.

Don't put all your eggs in one basket!

• Questions

1. What are the advantages playing golf would have over playing football?
2. What are some of the obstacles toward becoming a professional football player or golfer?
3. Do you think Jason's goals are realistic? Explain your answer.

LESSON 08 I Like Sports

Answer Me

- ### 3 The Hardest Sport?

    Chris : What do you think the hardest sport is?

    Ruth : I don't know. I guess the marathon. Marathoners have to be able to run for many hours just to finish the race.

    Chris : That's true, but they're very specialized. All they have to be able to do is run for long distances. Mainly, they just need a lot of endurance, but no special skills.

    Ruth : OK, I see your point. So what do you think is the hardest?

    Chris : The triathlon.

    Ruth : What's that?

    Chris : It's a race that combines three very different kinds of athletic ability, swimming, cycling, and running.

    Ruth : Wow! That must be hard!

    That's why we call them ironmen!

- ### Questions

    1. What sports do Chris and Ruth think are the hardest?
    2. How are the two sports different?
    3. What sporting event do you think is the hardest of all?

4 A Sound Mind In A Sound Body

Marvin : Let's go swimming.

Rhonda : Later, I'm busy now.

Marvin : You're just reading a book.

Rhonda : I know. But this is a kind of exercise.

Marvin : What are you talking about? How can reading be exercise? You don't even move!

Rhonda : It's a kind of mental exercise. We all need to have a good balance between our physical and mental training.

Marvin : OK, I agree with that. But you don't do any physical activity at all. Your face is always buried in a book.

Rhonda : And you never crack open a book at all. All you ever want to do is go swimming or hiking.

Marvin : Hmmm. Maybe we're both too one-sided.

Rhonda : I think you're right. I'll tell you what. I'll go swimming with you every day if you promise to read one book a week.

Marvin : It's a deal!

In balance.

Questions

1. What aspects of the human body should be kept in balance? Why?
2. Which part does Marvin over-emphasize? How about Rhonda?
3. How do they each agree to become more rounded?

LESSON 08 I Like Sports

— Let's Talk More —

1 Is It Fair?

Did you hear how much that young basketball player is going to make a year? It's millions of dollars! He'll probably be able to earn at least that much for a decade or longer—maybe even twenty years or more! I don't understand how anyone can be worth that much money, but especially not someone who doesn't really work for a living—he's being paid to play games! I love basketball and play every weekend, but I don't think it's very important except as good exercise and a way to relax. Playing basketball certainly doesn't fight poverty or improve health standards or make people more honest or better-educated. And the people who are actually trying to do some good in the world have trouble earning a living!

I wish I were more like you.

Questions

1. What would be a fair income for a professional athlete to make? Why do you think so?
2. What kind of job deserves the highest salary?
3. What are the good aspects of athletics? Are there any bad aspects?

Chat Room for Teens 01

• 2 Mind Games

I'm puzzled about the new trend of calling games like chess, cards, and go "brain sports." That just confuses two very different kinds of activities. In my opinion, a sport has to entail some sort of physical activity, such as running or swimming. Or it has to contain some sort of physical skill like archery. These so-called "brain sports" are very important and even exciting, and they're just as competitive as physical sports, but they shouldn't be called by the same name. They're just too different from each other.

Hard to learn, hard to play, but so much fun!

• Questions

1. What is the complaint over calling poker a "brain sport"?
2. According to the paragraph, what should be the criteria for calling some activity a "sport"?
3. Should yachting competitions or equestrian events be labeled "sports"? How about auto racing?

LESSON 08 I Like Sports

Let's Talk More

• 3 Going Pro

The difference between amateur and professional sports used to be very clear: whether or not people were paid to play them. But the lines became very blurred. "Amateur" athletes were, in effect, being paid to play college sports by getting a free education and free room and board, as well as other benefits. Some countries were heavily subsidizing their best athletes, in effect giving them salaries even though those countries pretended they were paying them for government "jobs" they were performing. In some sports, "amateur" athletes were getting rich by becoming celebrity "actors" or "models" and endorsing various products. So, nowadays, it's very hard to make any distinction between the pros and the non-pros. Even the Olympics, which for a century prided itself on excluding professionals, has abandoned that pretense, especially in competitions like basketball and tennis.

When sport becomes a paycheck, players may lose their passion for it.

• Questions

1. Technically, what is the difference between amateur and professional sports?
2. Name some ways in which that distinction became lost.
3. Why would anyone want to dedicate himself or herself to excel in an extremely difficult task if he or she weren't being paid for it?

Chat Room for Teens 01

• 4 Big Deal

What's the big deal about the Olympics? People spend many hours a day every week for years developing their skills, just to participate in an Olympic event once in their lives. Oftentimes, their governments give them huge financial incentives for winning (and they pay for their training as well), if they "bring home the gold." Many excellent athletes, even those who have consistently defeated their rivals in other competitions over many years and have set world records in their sport, are made to feel like failures if they have never won an Olympic gold medal. I feel that there is too much emphasis on this single sporting occasion and not nearly enough attention paid to the feats of courageous, selfless athletes during the four years between Olympic events.

Records exist to be broken.

• Questions

1. What does an athlete have to do to get into the Olympics?
2. If a sportsman doesn't win a gold medal in the Olympics, how is he treated?
3. How do governments encourage this attitude toward the Olympics?

LESSON 08 I Like Sports

— Real Talk —

You're On

Jeff : He did it! He scored!

Dad : I don't believe it! We were safely ahead just a moment ago, with time running out. And now the game's tied!

Jeff : Don't worry, Dad. My team isn't going to settle for a tie. They're going to win the game for sure!

Dad : No, they won't. My team's got the ball now. There's no way they can lose.

Jeff : Do you want to bet?

Dad : OK, I'll bet. If your team wins, I'll get you a new football. If my team wins, you have to wash the car.

Jeff : You're on!

Dad : Oh, no! Not a penalty! That stupid referee!

Jeff : The ref's just doing his job.

Dad : But it's just a momentary setback. Even though your team has the ball now, they're not going to score again. The game's almost over.

Jeff : But, never fear, we're still going to win — I told you!

Dad : What? You scored again so soon? How is that possible? I can't believe it.

Jeff : And now the game's over! We won 3-2. I told you!

Dad : Oh, I feel terrible. How could this happen?

Jeff : We've just got a better team than you, that's all. Let's go out and buy that football now.

• Questions

1. At the beginning of the dialog, what was the score?
2. Why doesn't Jeff have to wash the car?
3. Who does his dad blame for his team's loss?

Chat Room for Teens 01

Read Me

Two Big Ones

The two greatest sports events in the world are the Olympic Games and the World Cup Football Championship. The Olympics were begun by the Greeks thousands of years ago. The games were so important that wars were suspended while they took place. The first games were related to speed, strength, and military skills, but when they were revived a century ago they were expanded to include dozens of other kinds of sports.

The World Cup is also an international event that takes place every four years. But it involves only one sport, rather than many. However, football (or soccer) happens to be the most popular sport in the world. Many men, and some women, are avid fans and watch the sport many times a week. This is very much unlike the games in the Olympics. Very few people pay much attention to those sports on a regular basis; but for a few weeks every four years, the Olympics is the most important entertainment event in the world.

Why don't we stop wars during the Olympics anymore?

● Questions

1. Name two ways in which the Olympics and the World Cup are different.
2. List two ways that they are alike.
3. What did the original Olympics consist of?
4. What was the most impressive scene in the last Olympics? In the last World Cup?

LESSON 09 We Got a New Car

— Warm-up Dialog —

Dad's Car

Ralph : Did you see our new car?

Betty : Is that it over there?

Ralph : Yes! Isn't it beautiful?

Betty : What happened to the old one?

Ralph : It just quit running yesterday, while Dad was driving it to work. Dad got really angry when the garage told him how much it would cost to repair, so he just bought a new one instead.

Chat Room for Teens

Betty : It's so huge.

Ralph : I've always wanted a luxury SUV. It sure beats that little compact we've had so long.

Betty : Wasn't it expensive?

Ralph : Sure, but Dad just borrowed a lot of money from the bank. What do you think about it?

Betty : I think it's too big and expensive. Even the cost for gasoline and insurance must be enormous, and I'm sure it makes a lot of pollution.

Ralph : Aw, you sound just like my mom. When Dad drove it home, she told him that fixing the old one would be a lot cheaper in the long run.

● Questions

1. What does "in the long run" mean?
2. What does Ralph think about his family's new car? Why?
3. What does Betty think about it? Why?

Pictures

1.

Q1: What do your parents think about current gas prices? Do they complain about the government's role in fuel prices?

Q2: Do they try to drive less? Or do they have a carefree attitude about the cost of driving?

Q3: Do they do anything to save money on gas? If so, what?

2.

Q1: Is this scene usual on weekends? How about weekdays?

Q2: How do your parents respond to this kind of traffic jam?

Q3: What do you do when there is a traffic jam?

3.

Q1: What is happening here?

Q2: Have you ever seen your parent drive after drinking?

Q3: What would you do if your parent tried to drive drunk?

Talk

4. **Q1:** What is the man doing wrong?

    Q2 What do your parents do if their phone rings while they are driving?

    Q3: It is claimed that talking on the phone while driving is as dangerous as driving drunk. What do you think? What is dangerous about it?

5.

    Q1: What do you think happened?

    Q2 How does this reaction to the accident affect the other cars on the road?

    Q3: Have you ever seen your parent argue with some other driver on the road? Describe what happened.

6. **Q1:** Describe what happened in the picture.

    Q2 What would you do if you saw this kind of event?

    Q3: Why do you think the driver is running away from the accident?

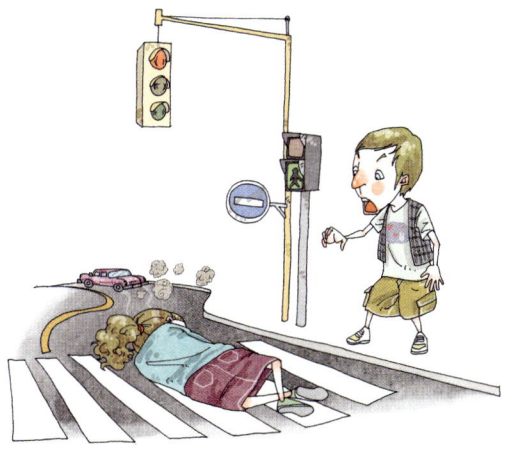

LESSON 09 We Got a New Car

Answer Me

1 The Best Choice

Dad : I'm going to buy a car today. Would you like to go along?

Mabel : What are you going to get?

Dad : I don't know yet. I'll see what's on the lot.

Mabel : You mean you aren't going to buy a new car?

Dad : No, I'm going to get a good used one. It's a lot cheaper.

Mabel : But a new car is guaranteed to work well.

Dad : No. New cars break down too, you know. But they have a warranty so they can be repaired for free.

Mabel : But what happens if you buy an old car and it breaks down.

Dad : Sometimes we can get warranties on used cars too. But we need to be careful about what we buy. If a car has been taken well care of, it should be as good as new for a long time.

Questions

1. With whom do you agree more, the father or the daughter?
2. Talk about why people buy used cars.
3. Do your parents buy new cars or used ones?

Chat Room for Teens 01

• 2 Status Symbol

Barry : Let's get a new car, Mom.

Mom : Why? Ours is only a couple of years old. It isn't even paid for yet.

Barry : I know. But we need a new one.

Mom : The one we have is in great shape. I don't think we need a new one.

Barry : But, Mom, Randy's dad just got a new luxury sedan. We can't let him think they're better than we are.

Mom : It takes a lot more than just a car to prove someone's worth.

Barry : I'd like to drive his big fat car into his smirking face!

Mom : Oh, you're just jealous.

• Questions

1. Does Barry's family need a new car?
2. Why does Barry think they do?
3. Will he be able to persuade his mother that he's right? Defend your answer.

LESSON 09 We Got a New Car

Answer Me

• 3 Running Lights

Mom : Watch out!

Dad : What?

Mom : You just ran a red light!

Dad : I know. But there wasn't anyone else coming.

Mom : We could have been killed.

Dad : No, we're perfectly safe. I made sure there weren't any other cars before I drove through it.

Mom : It doesn't matter. The light's there to protect us. If everybody ignored it like you did, nobody would ever be safe.

Dad : Well, we're late. I'm just trying to save some time.

Mom : The minute or so you might save, while endangering us and the other drivers, really wouldn't make any difference, would it?

Red lights don't count when you're alone!

That's how people get killed!

• Questions

1. Who do you think is right? Why?
2. Do your parents break the traffic rules when they are in a hurry? Do they drive too fast? Do they run through red lights? Explain in detail.
3. Have your parents ever been stopped by a cop for breaking the law? What happened?

Chat Room for Teens 01

● 4 Buckle Up

Dad : How many times do I have to tell you? Buckle up!

Sharon : But you never do.

Dad : I'm a lot bigger than you are. The belt is too tight for me.

Sharon : It's uncomfortable for me, too. But why should you be comfortable if I can't?

Dad : Because I'm driving. And I'm your father. So I have to be responsible for the safety and well-being of my passengers and my family as well.

Sharon : That doesn't mean it's fair.

Dad : All right, I'll tell you what. From now on, we'll both fasten our seatbelts. Every time! OK?

You buckle up too!

● Questions

1. Do your parents always buckle up? Why or why not?
2. Do you always fasten your seat belt even when you are in the back? Why or why not?
3. Give some reasons why we should buckle up.

LESSON 09 We Got a New Car

— Let's Talk More —

• 1 The Joneses

My father drives a compact car even though our neighbors all have sedans. He said that he isn't concerned about keeping up with the Joneses. When I asked him what that means, he said that too many people are only interested in status symbols. They want to own expensive, fashionable things because they want everyone else to think that they are important. He said he knows that he's important in all the meaningful ways that have nothing to do with money, so he doesn't feel the necessity of falsely impressing the others.

• Questions

1. Compared to a compact, what does owning a sedan seem to imply?
2. Instead of saying "keeping up with the Joneses," what other expression could you use?
3. What "meaningful ways that have nothing to do with money" do you think he is talking about?

Chat Room for Teens 01

• 2 Protectionist

These days I see many imported cars on the road. I wonder why. Most of them cost a lot more than cars made here. But are they really any better? I guess I could agree that someone might be willing to spend a small fortune for the very best car in the world, even if it was made abroad, but I don't see why anyone would do that for a pretty ordinary vehicle. And I sure don't understand how buying foreign cars helps make our own economy stronger.

What are your criteria for the best choice?

• Questions

1. What do you think is the best car in the world? Where is it made?
2. Why do some people want to buy foreign cars?
3. Why are there so many different kinds of cars on the road?

LESSON 09 We Got a New Car

— Let's Talk More —

• 3 Bike Safety

I like to ride my bike. I ride it every day if I can. But it is dangerous to ride it on the road by my house because there are too many cars. I'm afraid that I'll have an accident. And my mom says that all the exhaust fumes they emit are dangerous to my health. So, I don't know where I can ride my bike safely.

Why am I so exhausted!

• Questions

1. What is the narrator's dilemma? Can it be resolved? How?
2. Name two reasons why it is dangerous for him to ride his bicycle.
3. Can you think of any other reasons why riding a bike might be dangerous?

4 Why Drive?

If more people used public transportation, we could protect our environment and keep our society cleaner. We could also save a lot of fuel. There wouldn't be as much need for places to park, so we could use the space for other purposes — more homes or even more trees! And instead of driving, we could relax while we traveled; we could read or even take a nap instead of having to worry about having an accident or being late. I'm sure that it would even be safer; we hardly ever hear about bus or train crashes, but cars get into wrecks every day.

Questions

1. Name one advantage that using public transportation has over driving a car. Name another....
2. Then, why do so many people still want to drive?
3. What are some disadvantages with public transportation?

LESSON 09 We Got a New Car

Real Talk

Another Auto

Mom : We need another car.

Dad : Why? We just got this one a year ago. Is something wrong with it already?

Mom : No, it's fine. We don't need to replace it.

Dad : I don't understand. Didn't you just say we needed to?

Mom : No, I said we need another car. Not a different car, just one more car.

Dad : But why? We're still paying for this one.

Mom : I know, but when you drive it to work I'm stuck at home. I still have to take the kids to school and then pick them up, and I have grocery shopping to do and lots of other errands. Having a car would be a lot more convenient than taking a bus or subway, and a lot cheaper than a taxi.

Dad : I don't think we can afford it right now. Why don't we wait until next year and then see if we can afford it?

Mom : That's what you say every year, and we still haven't bought one.

Dad : We don't really need a new car. You just want one because all your female friends have a second car.

Mom : No, I do need one. Why don't you leave the car at home and you can take the subway to work? That'll solve our problem.

Dad : No, that would solve your problem! Then I'd have to get another car for my use. I have to have a car to do my job.

Mom : Then that settles it. We definitely need a second car.

As "one car per person" becomes standard, the concept of "family car" is a thing of the past.

● Questions

1. What is the difference between "another car" and a "different car?"
2. Why does the family need a second car?
3. Does the mother persuade her husband that she's right? How?
4. Does your family have a second car? Why?

Chat Room for Teens 01

Read Me

Rules Matter

Why should everybody keep traffic rules? Cars are heavy, fast, and dangerous. Around the world, thousands of people die in automobile accidents every year. Most of these accidents are preventable, if people would consistently follow the rules of the road. These rules regulate speed, direction, and right of way. If they did not exist, everyone would feel free to go anywhere, any time, and at any speed that he or she wants to. The result would not only be mass confusion but also a lot more fatalities, injuries, and property damage.

To keep the rules or not to keep the rules, that's the question!

● Questions

1. What do traffic rules do?
2. Why are they necessary? What would happen without the rules?
3. Are they always obeyed? Say why you think they are or are not.

Chat Room for Teens 01

LESSON 10 Let's Go Shopping

— Warm-up Dialog —

Same Thing?

Mom : Do you want to go to the department store with me? We need a new refrigerator.

Chuck : I'd love to go, if we can stop off in the computer game section before we come home.

Mom : OK. But we're not going to buy any more computer games!

Chuck : I just want to look around. Why are you buying a refrigerator in a department store? Isn't everything there more expensive?

Mom : Well, sometimes. But there are good reasons, especially for big-purchase items like a refrigerator.

Chuck : Such as?

Mom : Well, for one thing, the quality is guaranteed, so I know I can get it fixed, or get a new one, if it doesn't work.

While you're at it, can you get me a new game?

Chat Room for Teens

Chuck : Don't the discount stores do that too?

Mom : Sometimes. But if I have to take it back, I have to pay someone to move it. It's just a lot easier to pay a little more at the beginning and save a lot of time and trouble later.

Chuck : Is there any other reason?

Mom : Well, I think it's just easier for me to buy something if there's a fixed price. I'm always afraid that if I haggle I'll get ripped off.

Chuck : So how much extra do you think you'll have to pay?

Mom : They're having a big sale, so I should save about 25%.

Chuck : Wow! That's a lot! I think we should invest a tiny bit of what we save in a new game.

Mom : I said no new games.

Chuck : But if I get one in the department store, the quality is guaranteed and I won't get ripped off. We can take it back for free!

● Questions

1. Define "ripped off."
2. Why does Chuck's mom want to buy a refrigerator at the department store?
3. What does Chuck want to get? How does he try to convince his mom?

Pictures

1.

- Q1: What is happening here?
- Q2 Who do you think will attract the most customers?
- Q3: If the two supermarkets continue to compete by offering lower prices, what do you think will happen?

2.
- Q1: Why do people shop at department stores even though the prices are higher?
- Q2 Do your parents shop at department stores? Why or why not?
- Q3: What do they usually buy there?

3.

- Q1: Define "convenience store."
- Q2 How often do you go there? What do you usually buy there?
- Q3: What do you think about the prices there?

Talk

4.
- Q1: Who are these people?
- Q2: Why are they selling things on the street?
- Q3: Why do people buy from them?

5.

- Q1: What is a "flea market?"
- Q2: What do you think about flea markets? Do you think they are a good idea? Why or why not?
- Q3: Have you ever bought or sold anything there?

6.
- Q1: Do you know what "organic food" means?
- Q2: Why do people shop at organic food markets?
- Q3: How about the prices there? Are they lower or higher than at a supermarket?

LESSON 10 Let's Go Shopping

— Answer Me —

- ### 1 Winning Combination

Margaret : Wow! It sure is hot today!
Jonathan : It sure is. It's too bad we can't go to the pool.
Margaret : I know. It's just too far away.
Jonathan : So what can we do to cool off?
Margaret : I don't know. But I'm also hungry.
Jonathan : Me, too. But I don't have any money. Do you?
Margaret : No. But I have an idea!
Jonathan : What is it?
Margaret : Let's go to the department store nearby!
Jonathan : Why?
Margaret : Well, we can go to the supermarket downstairs. They always have free samples to eat.
Jonathan : And it's air conditioned as well! What a brilliant idea!

Can we get seconds?

- ### Questions

1. Do you think Margaret has a good idea?
2. Do you often sample free food at the supermarket? What kind?
3. Do you feel guilty about eating the free food if you don't buy anything there?

Chat Room for Teens 01

• 2 Fashion Sense

Doug : That's a nice dress you're wearing. Is it new?

Anna : Yes. I just got it yesterday. But I think it's ugly.

Doug : I think you look good in anything you wear.

Anna : But it isn't what the other girls are wearing! It just isn't cool.

Doug : If you hate it so much, why did you get it?

Anna : I didn't! My mom got it for me. But she never lets me choose what I want.

Doug : My mom buys all of my clothes too. But I don't mind.

If you like it, you should wear it, not me!

• Questions

1. Who buys your clothes?
2. If your parents buy your clothes, do you usually like what they get you?
3. If you buy your own clothes, do your parents usually like what you get?

LESSON 10 Let's Go Shopping

Answer Me

- **3 Why Dad Is Needed**

    Mom : Are you ready?
    Dad : Ready for what?
    Mom : We're going shopping.
    Dad : Oh, yeah. I forgot.
    Mom : Hurry up and get ready.
    Dad : I'd rather not go.
    Mom : Oh, come on. You need to get out of the house.
    Dad : You'll spend hours looking at clothes, and I'll get bored.
    Mom : I need your good advice about whether I should buy something or not.
    Dad : Oh, you never listen to my opinion anyway.
    Mom : Today I will, I promise. But I insist that you go along with me.
    Dad : OK, I'll go. But why is it so important?
    Mom : I need you to carry the things I buy. That way you won't be so bored!

    I didn't know you just wanted a pack horse when we married!

- **Questions**

    1. Do your parents ever shop together? Where do they go?
    2. What does your father think about going shopping with your mother?
    3. What about you? Do you usually go along with your parents when they shop? Do you enjoy it?

Chat Room for Teens 01

• 4 Home Shopping

Jennifer : Where are you going, Dad?

Dad : I'm going to get a TV. It's time we got one of the big new ones. Do you want to come along?

Jennifer : Why bother going out? Why don't you just shop at home, on the internet?

Dad : Because I don't trust it. I want to be able to see the TV for myself. If I buy online, I never know what I'm going to get.

Jennifer : But it's such a waste of time! You have a bigger selection online than you'll have in any single store, and you can usually get a better price too.

Dad : Maybe I'm old-fashioned, but I'd rather make physical contact with the seller and the product too. A picture of an item is never the same as the real thing.

Jennifer : OK. But I'm going to stay at home.

Old habits die hard!

• Questions

1. What do you think is wrong with the old TV?
2. What are some advantages of buying online?
3. What are some advantages of shopping in person?
4. Do your parents often buy online? What do they buy?

LESSON 10 Let's Go Shopping

— Let's Talk More —

1 Malls Have It All

It is no wonder that people go to the shopping mall so often. When it is hot outside, it's always cool there. And when it's cold, it's warm inside. When it is raining, shoppers can go there without getting wet or needing to carry an umbrella. And it is full of fashionable stores, delicious restaurants, and newly released movies, so shopping is fun even for people who don't want to buy anything.

I found Utopia!

Questions

1. How often do you and your parents go to a shopping mall?
2. What do you usually buy there?
3. What is the main reason for going there?

Chat Room for Teens 01

• 2 On Credit

It's very nice to be able to buy something now and pay for it later. That way you don't have to carry around a lot of money, and you only have to make one payment a month. And if you pay off the whole credit card balance at once, you won't have to pay more for the item than if you had paid for it with cash. But the problem is that most people are not careful enough. They buy more than they need or can easily afford, because it is so easy to charge it. But then when the credit card bill is due, they can't pay it all. So the rest of the bill is carried over to the next month for payment — at extremely high interest rates. So debt is piled on top of debt every month, and the charged items end up costing a lot more than they would have otherwise.

Credit Dominos

• Questions

1. What is an advantage of paying for things on credit?
2. What is a disadvantage?
3. How can people avoid the problems associated with credit cards?

LESSON 10 Let's Go Shopping

Let's Talk More

• 3 Stress Relief

My aunt is always complaining about stress. She says that her job and her family are too much to handle. But she makes up for it by going shopping. Every weekend she shops all day. Sometimes she spends a lot of money shopping. She buys clothes that she never wears and other things she never uses. When I asked her why she buys so much useless junk, she said that shopping is a way of relieving her stress. But to me, if I followed her "shop-till-you-drop" philosophy, I'd be under a lot more stress!

Oops! I bought too much to carry!

• Questions

1. What does "Shop till you drop" mean?
2. Do you think shopping helps reduce stress?
3. What about eating? Does it lessen stress too?
4. What is the best way to relieve stress?

4 Slashing Prices

Stores that have frequent promotions by slashing prices often find that the strategy may backfire. If consumers think that they can get a better deal later on if only they wait a little longer to buy, they will usually delay buying unnecessary items, and the store will not be able to make a satisfactory profit. For instance, my mom seldom buys clothes or electronics goods if they are not on sale. She gets a wonderful deal, of course, but the economy on the whole suffers.

Questions

1. Why do stores offer big discounts on products?
2. What is the risk in doing so?
3. Do you think stores charge too much for their goods anyway, so that even when they discount them they are still making a big profit?

LESSON 10 Let's Go Shopping

Real Talk

Shopping With Mom

Ken : I thought we came here to get groceries.

Mom : We did, but while I'm here I thought I should visit the women's department and find a new dress.

Ken : But we've been here an hour while you keep trying on clothes. Don't you like any of them?

Mom : Yes, I like them a lot. But I'm only going to get one. I want to make sure it's exactly right.

Ken : But I'm bored. And hungry. There's nothing to do here.

Mom : Don't worry, I'm almost done.

Ken : That's what you said fifteen minutes ago.

Mom : Hush. Just be patient, and we'll get a hamburger in a minute.

Ken : Let's go now.

Mom : If you're going to complain like this, next time I won't bring you.

Ken : Good! It isn't any fun for me to go shopping with you. If I stayed home I could watch television.

• Questions

1. Did Ken's Mom go shopping for groceries? Defend your answer.
2. Describe Ken's attitude.
3. What would Ken rather do?
4. Have you had any similar experience? Describe it.

Chat Room for Teens 01

Read Me

Shopaholism

Everyone knows what an alcoholic is: a person who drinks too much and cannot control his or her behavior. So, it follows that a "shopaholic" would be someone who shops addictively and can't help himself or herself. The more that person shops, the more shopping he or she needs to do! It's not a question of buying food because one is hungry, or clothes to keep oneself warm. The only thing that matters is the buying experience itself, not the product being purchased. The shopaholic goes from store to store in a frenzy, caring little or nothing about the value of the goods or whether they are reasonably priced, but only wants to get an emotional high by buying them. But, of course, that high wears off immediately, and the process needs to be repeated again and again. Just as with alcoholics, many shopaholics may go for a very long time without causing serious damage to themselves. But eventually, in both cases, the behavior leads to extremely dangerous results, financially and emotionally.

Everything comes to me!

• Questions

1. In your own words, what is a shopaholic?
2. What are the symptoms of shopaholism?
3. What serious financial and emotional problems could result?

DISCUSSION TEXTBOOK
FROM LIS KOREA

중고급 어린이 들을 위한 독창적인 영어교재

New Children's Talk (1), (2), (3)

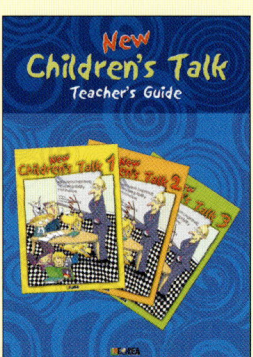

교사용

New Children's Talk (TG)

- 일상생활에서 벌어지는 상황들을 다양한 포맷에 맞추어서 많은 Speaking Chance를 제공합니다.
- 암기 위주의 영어가 아니라 자기 의견을 만들어 낼 수 있는 포맷들을 제공합니다.

본격적인 비지니스 토론 교재

Let's Talk Business
Major New Edition

15년 만에 새롭게 바뀐 Let's Talk Business -Major New Edition-의 특징은 다음과 같습니다.

- 현재 정보화 시대에 중요한 30개의 대표 이슈들을 선정했습니다.
- 각 이슈들은 Topic preview와 Warm-up Dialog에 의해 가볍게 다루어 지며, 또한 그림과 그림에 대한 가벼운 설명으로 독자들의 흥미를 이끌어 냅니다.
- 후에 각 이슈들은 전문적인 분석으로 상세하게 다루어지며, 이후 200개 이상의 질문으로 독자들의 의견을 이끌어 내게 됩니다.
- Current Hot Topic 섹션에서는 각 이슈에 대한 보충 이슈를 다루게 되며, 다시 한번 질문을 주어 독자들의 상상력을 자극합니다.

DISCUSSION TEXTBOOK
FROM LIS KOREA

자유토론을 위한 훈련과정
Talk Talk Talk (1), (2)

- Express Yourself / Let's Talk / What Do You Think? 과정을 무리 없이 이수하기 위한 예비단계로서 자유토론에 대비하기 위한 많은 훈련과정을 포함하고 있다.
- 여러 상황에 맞는 다양한 질문을 학생들에게 던짐으로써 질문과 응답들의 패턴을 이해하고 습득하게 하고자 했다.
- Express Yourself / Let's Talk / What Do You Think?의 주요 훈련 목표 중 하나인 어떤 영어 단어나 문장을 토론자 스스로 다시 설명하는 훈련에 중점을 두었다.

Talk Talk Talk의 선생님 교재
Teacher's Guide for Talk Talk Talk 1 & 2

- 기존에 출간 되었던 당사의 교재 Talk Talk Talk 1, 2의 선생님 교재로 출간 되었습니다.
- Talk Talk Talk 1, 2에 나왔던 모든 질문에 대한 정확한 답변과 필요한 경우 찬반 의견들이 모두 제시되어있습니다.

DISCUSSION TEXTBOOK
FROM LIS KOREA

토론교재의 베스트셀러
EXPRESS YOURSELF (1), (2), (3)
3rd Edition

- 토론 영어교재의 베스트셀러 Express Yourself 1/2/3 시리즈가 새롭게 출간되었습니다. 각 권 15개의 이슈를 깊이 있게 다루고 있으며, 다양한 토론주제와 Opinion Samples를 제공하고, 연관 dialog를 첨부하여 주제에 대한 이해력을 배가 시켰습니다.
- Points to Ponder 섹션에서는 다양한 의견들이 나올 수 있는 주제를 제시하여 다양한 토론이 되도록 했습니다.
- 토론주제와 연결되는 다양한 수백 개의 그림과 더불어 캡션을 덧붙여서 미국영어의 재미와 아름다움을 느끼도록 하였습니다.

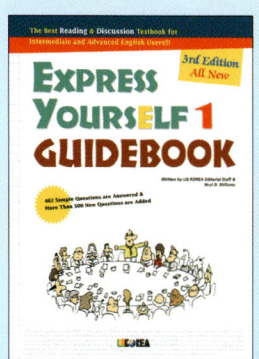

토론교재의 베스트셀러
EXPRESS YOURSELF (1)
Guidebook
3rd Edition

본 Express Yourself 1 Guidebook은
- 첫째, 각 이슈에 제공된 대표 질문들에 대하여 다양한 의견들을 제시하여 독자들이 각각의 의견을 표출하는데 도움이 되도록 했습니다.
- 둘째, Express Yourself 1의 각 이슈에 제시된 Points to Ponder의 의미를 영어로 자세히 설명함으로써 독자들의 이해를 돕고자 했습니다.
- 셋째, 여기에 제시된 다양한 의견들에 대하여 또 다른 질문을 더 함으로써 독자들의 상상력과 의견 표출 능력을 높이고자 하였습니다.

DISCUSSION TEXTBOOK
FROM LIS KOREA

 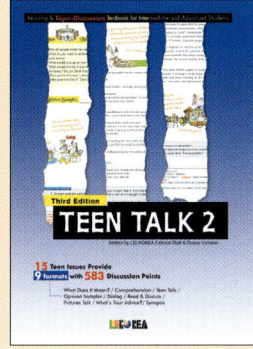

청소년을 위한 토론교재
New Teen Talk (1), (2)

- 청소년 토론교재의 최고 높은 단계의 교재로서 각 권 15개의 이슈 속에 500개 이상의 토론주제를 제시합니다.
- 각 권에 포함된 9개의 포맷은 (What Does It Mean? / Comprehension / Teen Talk / Opinion Samples / Dialog / Read & Discuss / Pictures Talk / What's Your Advice? / Synopsis) 각각의 특징에 맞는 다양하고 흥미로운 토론 주제를 제공합니다.

중급자들을 위한 토론교재
Speak Your Mind (1), (2)

- 일상적이며 쉬운 주제들을 선정하여 간결하게 정리했음.
- 대표 주제에 대한 질문과 대답을 여론조사 형식으로 꾸며 독자들이 쉽게 주제에 접근할 수 있도록 했음.
- 모든 주제들에 찬반 의견을 달아 독자들의 다양한 의견을 접할 수 있도록 했음.

Chat Room for Teens ❶

초판 4쇄 인쇄 : 2023년 1월 05일 인쇄
초판 4쇄 발행 : 2023년 1월 10일 발행
지 은 이 : 리스코리아 편집부
          & Duane Vorhees
펴 낸 곳 : (도서출판) 리스코리아
펴 낸 이 : 조은예
등   록 : 남양주 제 399-2011-000003호
전   화 : 0502-423-7947
일러스트레이터 : 김기환
편 집 디 자 인 : 예림칼라
인   쇄 : 더블비

www.liskorea.com

All rights reserved. No part of this book may be reproduced, stored in a retrieval system, or transmitted in any form or by any means, electronic, mechanical, photocopying, recording or otherwise, without the prior permission in writing of the Publisher.